Preface

Looking at where we started, it brings great joy to be bringing you the second edition of Your Complete Guide to Organic Poultry Farming. We have come a long way from the First edition to this very one, and I want to take this time to appreciate everyone who bought the first edition of this book. My special thanks to those who took out time to write detailed comments and contributions – those feedback is like fuel in the gasoline engine.

If you are just coming across organic poultry farming, then you should count yourself lucky to be coming in when there is even a lot more on the table – just for you.

Personally, I must say that, having practiced organic poultry farming for the past few years, I only wish I had started earlier. We started quite well but have also learned a lot more in the process, which is why I bring you this second edition – a fuller dose.

As always, DiY Agric Consult is committed to teaching you, in a step-by-step manner, how to do it yourself, and this second edition is no exception.

So, let's see how we have moved from a people who drifted away from the organic way to becoming a large community of farmers who are insanely committed to making sure that organic poultry farming is widely embraced.

Disclaimer

This book has been published for the purpose of enlightening the reader and sharing knowledge about organic poultry farming based on the author's experience. The claims herein, except otherwise stated, are used to guide the reader in taking actions related to organic poultry farming. The publisher/author will in no wise be liable to any loss or failure of procedures or processing resulting from user's negligence, error, or misunderstanding of the information. The reader is responsible for the benefits and any loss incurred in the course of following the guide. In other words, you are responsible for your own choices, actions and results.

Copyright © 2020 by Opeyemi Afeluyi

All rights reserved. No part of this publication may be reproduced, distributed, or transmitted in any form or by any means, including photocopying, recording, or other electronic or mechanical methods, without the prior written permission of the publisher, except in the case of brief quotations embodied in critical reviews and certain other noncommercial uses permitted by copyright law. For permission requests, write to the publisher, addressed "Attention: Permissions Coordinator," at the address below.

guidefreakblog@gmail.com

Bringing you everything you need to do it yourself

ORGANIC POULTRY FARMING 101

The concept of Organic Poultry farming is not so hard to understand. But, if this statement is true, why are farmers not practicing organic poultry farming in spite of its benefits? My answer is, you don't practice what you do not know or understand.

I want to congratulate you for laying your hands on this e-book because it's about to help you understand organic poultry farming in ways that you can expand by yourself. Here, in this e-book, I will explain what organic poultry farming is and why you can practice it effectively.

Just so I am clear, Organic poultry farming is the rearing of chickens for meat or eggs under a sustainable culture without the use of antibiotics, hormones or other synthetic drugs. There are other factors that also set the organic chicken apart from any other chicken. But before we dive into more details, I would like to say that the benefits of organic poultry farming are enormous and worth exploring. So, I promise you that it's going to get even more interesting as you continue to read.

DiY Agric © 2020

CONDITIONS FOR ORGANIC POULTRY FARMING

You don't want to open your mouth to say that you have raised your chickens organically if some conditions are not met. So, I am going to make a list of some of those conditions that have to be met.

1. ZERO ANTIBIOTICS

If you ask me, I would say that this is the most important factor that sets the organic chicken apart. Also, it is the area where farmers fail to adhere to. Before the practice of poultry farming can be termed organic, the farmer must abstain from the use of antibiotics, drugs, and hormones. As a matter of fact, a chicken stops being organic the moment it is given a synthetic drug. One might ask, why the fuss about the use of antibiotics on chickens. This is because most of the antibiotics administered to chickens are similar to the ones that are used by humans.

In case you are yet to get the message, I will explain further. These antibiotics often leave residues in chickens, and when the chickens are consumed by humans, the residues are ingested as well. Consequently, it encourages bacteria in the body to develop resistance to those antibiotics, such that when they are administered to humans in treatment doses, there are bacteria strains that can easily resist the treatment.

2. ORGANIC POULTRY INVOLVES ACCESS TO PASTURE

This is next to the use of antibiotics. While you have to deprive your organic chickens from antibiotics for prevention and treatment of diseases, you need to allow them access to pasture. You may not know this, but some pasture plants and herbs have natural antibiotic properties to help ward off diseases from your chickens. At this point, I would like to state that pasture-raised chickens are not necessarily organic chickens. If they have a dose of antibiotics at any stage in their life, they cease to be organic chickens. To embrace this culture of pasture, organic poultry farming is not complete if the birds are confined in cages without access to pasture.

3. EXCLUSIVELY ORGANIC FEED

Chickens raised under organic poultry farming are fed exclusively with organic feed, including whole grains and supplements. It is very important to note that the growing of the grains used in organic poultry farming cannot be done with genetic modification.

CAN THESE CONDITIONS FOR ORGANIC POULTRY FARMING BE MET?

In my opinion, farmers should find it easy to obey conditions #2 and #3. However, condition #1 seems to be a no-go area if the farmer is not equipped with the knowledge of controlling diseases in the organic way. But again, I will say "CONGRATULATIONS" to you because you now have what it takes to defend your flock from those diseases that may force antibiotics into your hands and make you compromise on your vow to go ORGANIC.

As a seasoned Animal Scientist with the knowledge of organic poultry farming, I have taken time to prepare this ultimate guide to organic poultry farming, and I cannot wait to start getting positive feedback from you all. I know you will soon jump for joy when you realize how easy it is to tackle even the most fearful poultry diseases with simple herbs and spices you have always had around you.

In my case, I was stunned when I first tried combating coccidiosis with ORDINARY bitter leaf. As a matter of fact, I had tried to destroy the giant bitter leaf tree in my compound but the tree would sprout again after some weeks. Thank God it never really died! Now I am doing my very best to have it in abundance, and would even condemn anyone who tries to mishandle the tree. Organic Poultry Farming has made me to value the things I once thought I could live without.

It is my earnest desire that this guide will not only show you organic poultry farming in a detailed form, but also show you EVERYTHING you need to succeed as an organic poultry farmer.

Very soon, you will be reading about the common herbs and spices that form a defense system for chickens and some safe organic growth hormones that you will get in plants for maximum growth of your chickens. This is big!

For gaining access to this book, you will also know how to prepare multivitamins and immune boosters with the common plants that you already know.

Everything will be step-by-step and easy to follow. Let's continue.

This guide combines my years of experience as a graduate animal scientist and the precious knowledge of organic poultry farming.

DiY Agric © 2020

THE NEED FOR HEALTHY GUT

This is an important aspect of your chickens' health that many people do not know or give attention to. A lot of farmers are interested in Indigenous Microorganisms IMO's, Lactobacillus (LAB), and feed fermentation but are ignorant of the chemistry or biochemistry behind these. Well, I will throw some light.

Permit me to inform you that every chicken's health largely depends on the state of its intestines. In other words, most of the diseases of a chicken propagate in or targets the intestines. This is the reason why a chicken's poop is a good way of judging if the chicken is well or otherwise.

As a farmer, if you are able to master the act of maintaining a healthy gut for your chickens, automatically, you will be arresting and preventing a lot of diseases. Although there are a couple of ways to maintain a healthy gut for your chickens, I will be talking about two of the most important procedures which are Feed fermentation and the use of Lactobacillus.

FEED FERMENTATION

First, let me show you some of the benefits of giving your chickens fermented feed.

1. Fermented feed is better absorbed in the chicken's gut
2. It provides your chickens with more nutrients
3. Fermented feed adds probiotics (beneficial bacteria) to your chickens' digestive health
4. Adds the B vitamins such as Niacin, Thiamin to your chickens
5. It improves your birds' immunity
6. It reduces overall cost of feeding as chickens
7. Reduces chicken waste

How To Ferment Poultry Feed

1. Get a plastic container that is larger than the volume of feed you want to ferment
2. Add your dry feed (Mash or grains) to fill maximum of 1/3 the space inside the bucket
3. Fill the bucket with water, ensuring that the dry feed is fully submerged and the water on top is a few inches over the top of the dry feed.
4. Make sure there is still enough space in the bucket to allow for swelling

5. Cover the bucket with a perforated lid to allow for gaseous exchange.
6. Turn the feed every 12 hours
7. Do this for 3 days and the fermentation process would be in a steady state.

At this stage, you can continue to serve the fermented feed to your chickens. To keep the cycle, just replace the amount of feed taken from the fermentation bucket with equal quantity of dry mash or grain, depending on the composition of initial feed. However, always return the drained water to ensure that the water in the fermented feed is over the level of the feed itself. Always keep the upper part of the bucket (where there is no water) clean to prevent unwanted growth and contamination.

DiY Agric © 2020

DEWORMING YOUR CHICKENS NATURALLY

The need to deworm chickens comes with the desire to get the maximum production from your birds. And deworming your chickens naturally means you will be cutting on your expenses, which is what every farmer wants. As an organic poultry farming enthusiast, myself, I am aware of various natural dewormers for chickens but I want to share the best. I will be showing you how to deworm chickens naturally using papaya (pawpaw) seeds powder

Why Use Papaya Seeds for Chickens

You might want to ask why I choose papaya seeds for chickens, and not any other substance that can be used to deworm chickens. Let me explain why:

Since the focus is to get a natural agent that can eradicate worms from chickens, First I find pawpaw seeds to stand out in efficacy. Research shows its ability to remove all roundworms and tapeworms that are capable of hindering your birds from growing well. With papaya seeds, you can get rid of all worms within 2-3 days of use.

Another reason for choosing pawpaw seeds is the fact that it is an agricultural waste. This means that it will cost you almost nothing to get. In my own case, I just have to approach the people slicing and selling pawpaw, and they always gave me with gladness. It's a waste product to them, but something of high value to me.

How to Know When to Use Papaya Seeds Powder

Papaya Seeds Powder (PSP)

There are some signs and indications that your chickens might be infested with worms. One prominent sign is slow growth and loss of appetite. It's almost like the worms are taking the food as your bird eats. Your chicken poop color and form can also serve as a pointer that they have worms and should be dewormed.

Also, since there is no adverse effect of using papaya seeds for chickens, you can deworm on a routine. Maybe once in a month.

How to Use Papaya Seeds to Deworm

You can now choose to give your chickens a healthy life by maximizing the use of every pawpaw tree close to you. If you are extracting your papaya seeds, you need to follow these steps to deworm your chickens naturally

- Slice a pawpaw into two halves
- Scoop out the seeds and wash to exclude the yellows
- Sun-dry the seeds until they are very dry
- Grind into powder
- It's as simple as that

Now to cure worms, you need to give 3 grams of the powder per kg live-weight of chicken. That is, if you have a chicken that is 3KG in weight, you need to administer 9 grams of the powder. You can do the Maths for as many chickens you have.

You should add the papaya seeds powder (PSP) to their feed for 2-3 days to deworm them naturally

Other benefits of This Method

- The papaya seeds powder (PSP) can be stored easily
- There is a definite dosage (3 grams per KG live weight of bird)
- It is cheap; you don't even have to buy anything
- It doubles as a cure for coccidioides
- You can also decide to add to water instead of feed.

DiY Agric © 2020

Intestinal worms stand to compete with your chickens for the nutrients in their body, hence they should be eliminated as quickly as possible. This is to ensure that your chickens reach market weight as at when due. The use of papaya seeds powder has been found to be highly effective in eliminating worms, and you can try it today.

NATURAL GROWTH PROMOTERS FOR BROILERS

When broiler farmers raise broiler chickens, there are three things on their mind. The first is how they can make sure that the broilers reach the highest possible weight in the shortest time possible. While there are options when it comes to the use of growth promoters for broilers, organic broiler growth promoters are safer. Usually, farmers adopt the use of Antibiotic Growth Promoters in broiler diet to help promote growth. Some of the dietary antibiotics used include Flavomycin, Zinc bacitracin, and Virginiamycin. Some studies claim that Virginiamycin is the most effective option among the three.

So that we don't shift the focus of this article, let me tell you why these dietary antibiotics may not be the best. It's simply because dietary antibiotics result in antibiotic resistance. This explains why NAFDAC has banned the inclusion of antibiotics in animal feed. In this article, I will unveil some natural/organic growth promoters that farmers are using to promote broiler growth. These are safer, cheaper, and do more than promote

DiY Agric © 2020

growth but also keep your chickens healthy. Alright, let me introduce to you some growth recipe.

1. Cloves as Natural Growth Promoter (Syzygium aromaticum)

Cloves are an ancient spice. They are one of the amazing natural supplements that you can use to achieve rapid growth in broiler farming. Cloves are effective as a growth promoter when you add to broiler feed at inclusions of 100 – 200 mg (0.1-0.2 g) per kg of feed. You can use a digital scale to measure your ingredients. Cloves can be used independently as a growth promoter or combined with other growth promoters. Apart from working as a growth promoter for broilers, cloves also have health benefits for broilers.

2. Black pepper (Piper nigrum) as Growth Promoter

Black pepper – iyere in Yoruba, uziza in Igbo, uda in Hausa, and urire in urhobo. This is another growth promoter that is worthy of mention. It is rich in minerals like zinc, potassium, calcium, manganese, iron, lycopene, carotene, magnesium, and zeazanthin. They are excellent sources of vitamin B complex groups such as pyridoxine, riboflavin, thiamin and niacin, which explains why it increases feed consumption in broiler chickens.

3. Cayenne Pepper/Hot Pepper (Capsicum annum)

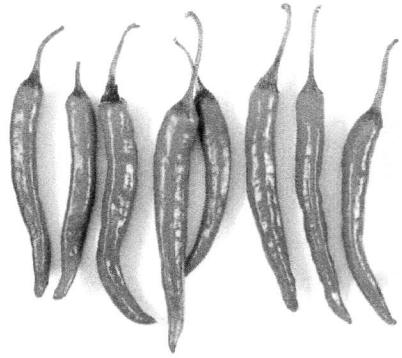

Amazingly, Cayenne pepper finds itself on the list of non-antibiotic growth promoters too. And just so you know, there are a lot of benefits that your broiler's gut will get from this hot spice. Cayenne or hot pepper will increase broiler feed intake so you might want to make it a part of your broiler diet. At an inclusion rate of 1.5 g/kg of feed, Cayenne does the job of a growth promoter so well, and you really should try it. You will also need a digital scale to measure the right proportion of cayenne per kg of feed. You can think of this as a worthy investment. I got mine on Amazon many years ago. What's more is that, at that inclusion rate, Cayenne pepper has no negative effect on the birds or their organs.

4. Bitter Kola as Broiler Growth Promoter (Garcinia kola)

No, we are not done yet! Who says broilers don't get something good out of bitters too? In addition to the antimicrobial effects of bitter kola, it has also been found to be a fantastic natural growth promoter that farmers can use to make their broilers attain impressive weights in the shortest time possible. So, if you are adding bitter kola to your broiler feed, you are at least sure that you have a good growth promoter and an antimicrobial agent in their feed.

How to use Bitter Kola as Broiler Growth Promoter

To use Bitter Kola as broiler growth promoter, sun-dry the seeds and grind them into powder. Add 25g per KG of feed

There is a lot to benefit from the use of organic growth promoters. Not only do they conveniently replace synthetic options, they have remarkable health benefits too. These four growth promoters are remarkable, and if I can discover them, I'm sure there has to be more.

UNDERSTANDING CHICKEN POOP (COLOR AND FORM)

Watery chicken poop, bloody, white, yellow, etc., are age-long signs that farmers use to monitor the heath of their chickens. However, to use this method, you must understand what a normal chicken poop looks like. Not only that, you need to know when and why chickens poop are bloody, white, green, black, yellow and watery chicken poop. If you have ever asked questions like:

- What does watery chicken poop mean?
- Why is my chicken poop watery?
- Why is my chicken poop bloody?
- And so on...

Then this article is help to answer those questions. I will be showing you how to treat diarrhea in chickens, coccidiosis in chickens and how to use the color and texture of chicken poops to diagnose their health.

Normal Chicken Poop

The truth about normal chicken poop is that there is no fixed color. It still depends on the diet and state of chicken's health. While the ash poop with white cap is generally assumed to be the normal chicken poop, several shades of colors can be normal too. However, these other colors should not persist for too long. If they do, then your chickens might be having some diseases. Unlike watery chicken poop, normal chicken poop is supposed to be firm.

Green Chicken Poop

If your chickens have been exposed to greens like vegetables or grasses, then a green chicken poop might just be based on diet. If you are sure that nothing that the chickens have eaten should cause the green poop, then you might want to consider some possible diseases.

Sometimes, the green poop might be watery chicken poop, and other times, they are firm. Your birds may be showing signs of Avian flu, Newcastle disease, Marek's disease, or the less scary probable cause – internal worms.

Suggested Treatment:

There is no need for treatment if the cause is dietary. However, if it is internal worms, you can use Ivermectin. Alternatively, use garlic and pawpaw seed as organic remedy for worms. In the case of viral causes like Newcastle disease, there is no synthetic cure. What should have been done is the administration of LaSota vaccine. You will also learn how to use Tagiri (Christmas melon for Newcastle disease) in this section

Yellow and Foamy Poop

This is sometimes noticed at the early stage of coccidiosis. It is a safe period to administer an effective coccidiostat to quick recovery. It can also be an indication of fowl typhoid or internal worm infestation.

Suggested Treatment:

For Coccidiosis, use drugs like Amprolium, Embazine Forte, Amprococ, or Tultrazuril. See how to use bitter leaf as an organic remedy for coccidiosis. For internal worms, use Ivermectin. Alternatively, use garlic and pawpaw seed as organic remedy for worms

Bloody Chicken Poop

Bloody poop can appear as watery chicken poops without any solid, and sometimes with the normal solid grey matter. Bloody poop is characteristic of coccidiosis and the amount of blood depends on the severity of the condition. Usually, chickens with severe cases of coccidiosis will not have appetite to eat. This is because coccidiosis takes its toll on the intestine of its victim.

Suggested Treatment:

Use drugs like Amprolium, Embazine Forte, Amprococ, or Tultrazuril. *See how to use bitter leaf as an organic remedy for coccidiosis.*

Brown Runny Chicken Poop

Sometimes, this is only a result of foods that are high in liquid. Hens will excrete this kind of poop a few times a day. If that is the case, then you have nothing to worry about.

However, runny brown poop can also be a sign of either Infectious bronchitis or E. coli infection. If so, you will have to treat your chickens pretty quickly.

Suggested Treatment:

Use strong antibiotics like oxytetracycline, erythromycin, gentatylo, etc. You can also see how to use garlic as an organic remedy for the condition.

White, Milky Chicken Poop

This can either be internal worms or a case of gumboro disease, also known as Infectious Bursal Disease. The former can be easily treated with a dewormer but the latter is a threat to any farmer.

Suggested Treatment:

Use Ivermectin for worm, but IBD should be prevented with Gumboro vaccine. Alternatively, you can use Tagiri (Christmas melon) for Organic prevention.

Clear or Watery Chicken Poop

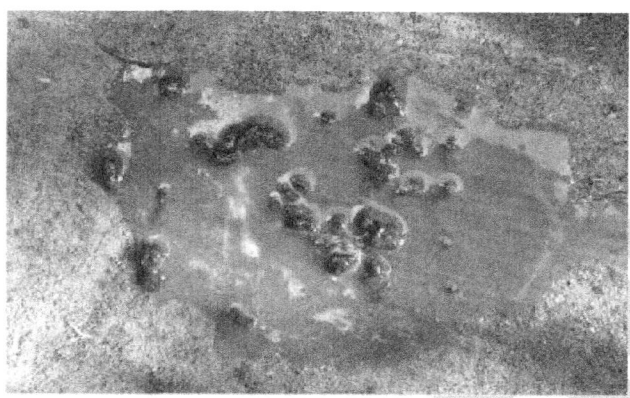

Usually, this can be a sign that your chickens have been stressed. It can be as a result of transportation, or they've been out of feed for a while.

Where watery chicken poop is a concern is when it is an indication of Infectious bronchitis.

Suggested Treatment:

You should use strong antibiotics to revive your chickens. You shouldn't have this problem if you usually include garlic and other organic body guards in your chicken diet.

Black Chicken Poop

If you are sure that your chickens have not been out to eat some dark apples or charcoal, then you might want to suspect internal bleeding. It could also be as a result of very high level of protein in your chicken feed. Another thing that could cause black Poop is when your hen is brooding and has not eaten for a while. She may pass out a big load of this dark watery poop but not as black as when it is internal bleeding.

Suggested Treatment:

For internal bleeding, administer vitamins. For high protein content in feed, manipulate your feed formula accordingly.

Verdict

This section is intended to help you diagnose the health condition of your chickens. It is also intended to help you answer those questions that come to mind when you suddenly see a strange poop in your chicken coop. However, if you are still not sure what might be wrong, you should take your chicken for a test.

ORGANIC MEDICATIONS

As you make up your mind to go all organic or try organic with a limited number of chickens, I have prepared this aspect of the guide to help you when diseases show up – because they will – someday. However, your confidence will be like an immovable mountain by the time you begin to practice everything in this guide.

As an animal science student then at the Federal University of Technology, Akure, I was happy with everything I learned but not as happy as I was when we began to talk about diseases and how to combat them - even the deadliest poultry diseases. This is partly because I had tried poultry farming on a small scale before I got my admission, and I can remember losing all but one of my chickens at a point. I hope that the organic medication aspect of my guide gives you the kind of confidence I have now.

The aim of the farmer when using organic medications is mainly to boost birds' immune system by administering herbs, spices, roots, fruits, leaves, etc., which have been prepared into concoction or to be used independently in various forms. The good news is that organic medication can take care of all poultry diseases, including viral diseases.

Some common ingredients are:

1. Lactic Acidic Bacteria (LAB) – a special probiotic
2. Super Tagiri (prepared from the Tagiri bulb)
3. Garlic
4. Ginger
5. Cayenne pepper
6. Habanero pepper
7. Bitter leaf
8. Turmeric
9. Black pepper
10. Aloe Vera
11. Carrots
12. Cucumber
13. Garden eggs
14. Egg shells
15. Pawpaw
16. Apple
17. Moringa
18. Neem leaf
19. Basil (Scent leaf)
20. Lime
21. Lemon and so many more

DiY Agric © 2020

Opeyemi Afeluyi

SPICES CHART

DiY Agric © 2020

As mentioned earlier, these organic ingredients are specially prepared. In some cases, the juice is extracted and required dosage is administered to the birds from day old to harvest time.

They can also be used for treatment and control of diseases in birds.

Like any other medication, administration of these organic medications can be done through water, feed, and in extreme cases orally. But do not worry, I will tell you how to do everything step-by-step.

However, the most preferred method is through their drinking water.

DISEASES ASSOCIATED WITH POULTRY, AND THEIR ORGANIC REMEDIES

As lucrative as the poultry business is, the problem of disease management has been a major threat to farmers' profit. However, there are safe and effective organic ways a farmer can prevent and control poultry diseases to limit the amount spent of diseases. The following are the major diseases challenging poultry business and the corresponding organic medications to combat them.

Newcastle Disease Virus (NDV)

Newcastle disease is a viral disease of poultry that can be prevented through effective organic medications and has also been proven to be organically curable.

Prevention is achieved by administering a combination of herbs, roots, leaves etc. These will be highlighted later in this guide.

Treatment of New Castle Disease (Experimental): The following table shows the ingredients that have been found effective in combating Newcastle disease. I have prepared the table to show the different measurements required for 400, 200, and 100 birds respectively. This should help you in your own calculation.

Ingredients	400 Birds	200 Birds	100 Birds
Cayenne pepper	340g	170g	85g
Aloe Vera gel	340g	170g	85g
Wood Ash	4 tbsp (57.2 g)	2 tbsp (28.6 g)	1 tbsp (14.3 g)
Water	4 Liters	2 Liters	1 Liter

The mixture should be administered like a vaccine to birds using the corresponding measurement

Infectious Bursa Disease (IBD) – A.K.A Gumboro

This is another viral disease of high economic impact, but the good news is that it also responds well to the same concoction use to combat Newcastle Disease. Therefore, when confronted with Gumboro, just get your Cayenne pepper, Aloe Vera, Wood Ash, and water, and mix in the proportion described in the table above.

DiY Agric © 2020

Marek Disease Virus (MDV)

Effective management of Marek Disease (Experimental): The following have been found to be effective in combating Marek disease

Ingredients	400 Birds	200 Birds	100 Birds
Cayenne pepper	340g	170g	85g
Aloe Vera gel	340g	170g	85g
Black pepper	340g	170g	85g
Water	4 Liters	2 Liters	1 Liter

The mixture should be administered like vaccine to birds with the corresponding measurement.

Coccidiosis

Coccidiosis is a poultry disease often characterized by bloody poop, sometimes brownish. It is a disease of high economic value especially in broiler production and should be handled as fast as possible.

Organic Treatment: Bitter leaf extract

- Gather some bitter leaves. The quantity depends on the volume of juice you are hoping to get and the number of chickens you want to treat.

- Remove the leaves from the stem and rinse them in a bowl. Be sure to rinse properly but don't squeeze too hard.
- Put the leaves in a kitchen blender and add just a little water. Just enough water to blend the leaves easily. What you need is a juice that is as thick as 5 Alive, so don't add too much water at this stage.
- Blend until the leaves are cut into tiny particles.
- Use a cheese cloth to sieve the juice into a container.
- If you have followed the process carefully, the bitter leaf extract should be as thick as 5 Alive.

  _Dosage__: 20ml per liter of water for prevention_
  30-40ml per liter of water for treatment (cure)

Diarrhea

Organic Treatment: Scent leaf + Bitter leaf extract

- Gather equal amount of scent leaves and bitter leaves. The quantity depends on the volume of juice you are hoping to get and the number of chickens you want to treat.
- Remove the leaves from the stem and rinse it in a bowl. Be sure to rinse properly but don't squeeze too hard.
- Put the leaves in a kitchen blender and add just enough water to blend the leaves easily. What you need is a juice that is as thick as 5 Alive, so don't add too much water at this stage.

- Blend until the leaves are cut into tiny particles.
- Use a cheese cloth to sieve the juice into a container.
- If you have followed the process carefully, the bitter leaf extract should be as thick as 5 Alive.

Dosage: 20ml per liter of water for prevention

30-40ml per liter of water for treatment (cure)

Salmonella

Organic Treatment: Clove + Ginger + Garlic extract + Scent leaves

- Blend 350 grams of cloves, ginger, and garlic
- Add 700 grams of Scent leaves
- Add 500 ml of water and blend together

Dosage: *30ml to a liter of water for 3-5 days*

E-coli

Organic Treatment: Clove + Ginger + Garlic extract + Scent leaves

- Blend 350 grams of cloves, ginger, and garlic
- Add 700 grams of Scent leaves
- Add 500 ml of water and blend together

Dosage: *30ml to a liter of water for 3-5 days*

Fowl Typhoid

Organic Treatment: Clove + Ginger + Garlic extract, Aloe Vera gel, and Cayenne pepper (dry)

For fowl typhoid, you need to get a liquid blend of each of the above ingredients except Cayenne pepper.

Dosage: Add 20ml of each and 2 tbsp of Cayenne pepper to a liter of water

Chronic Respiratory Disease (CRD)

This is a terrible respiratory disease that is most commonly found in broilers. It interferes with the normal breathing of infected birds and can be very fatal. It often comes with signs like chirping or labored breathing. There are also symptoms of cough.

Organic Treatment: Ginger + Garlic extract + Cayenne pepper (dry)

- Get 350 grams each of Ginger and Garlic
- Blend in 500 ml of water
- Administer 20ml per liter to their drinking water, adding 2 tbsp of powdered cayenne pepper to every litter.

Dosage: 20ml to a liter of water, Cayenne pepper 2 tbsp to a liter of water

Fowl Pox

To treat Fowl Pox, scrape black spots with blade, clean surface with lime or lemon, apply palm oil on surface and then give affected bird palm oil or honey to drink (give orally)

Coryza

Organic Treatment: Ginger + Garlic + Turmeric

To treat Coryza, you should get a liquid blend of each of the above ingredients and add 20ml of each to 1 liter of water.

Dosage: (20ml each into 1 liter of water)

Worms

Organic Treatment: Garlic + Ginger + Pawpaw seeds or refer to the section on deworming with papaya

Prolapse

Prolapse is when a part of a hen's oviduct comes out through the anus usually during egg laying and refuses to retract. This is common in young laying hens, especially when they are not allowed to develop properly during the rearing stage before they start to lay.

To avoid this or reduce its occurrence, you must allow your pullets to grow as recommended by the hatchery. Also, excessive lighting is not suitable for young layers.

To treat prolapse, wash the distended oviduct with warm water, push it back inside, and apply honey to allow for quick tightening of the area.

You can also give the hen a blend of Garlic extract + Cayenne pepper (20ml per liter)

PREPARATION OF MULTIVITAMINS CALCIUM AND OTHER MULTIVITAMINS

Have you ever wondered why some chickens cannot stand to their feet, and why some broilers after attaining a good weight will not be able to work well? If you can prepare your Multivitamins Calcium, you should be done with that problem for life. YES!

Beyond helping your birds to grow strong bones, this purely organic supplement is also effective in correcting some bone defects in chicks. You will soon find out! Let's see what you need to prepare you own calcium supplement.

Ingredients:

1. Garden eggs
2. Carrots
3. Cucumbers
4. Egg shells
5. Water
6. Molasses

Get a good quantity of all the items mentioned in the same proportion except the egg shells and molasses. Let's now get into the process.

- You need to first cut the ingredients into small cuts
- Grind or blend all the ingredients into a thick paste gradually adding little water as you blend
- Pour all into a big bucket and add chlorine-free water twice its volume, (not chlorinated water)
- Stir and cover with a breathable, mesh and hold with a rubber band
- Try to prevent external particles from entering.
- Keep in a clean environment and away from sunlight
- Allow the content to stay for 72 hours
- Stir every 12 hours (twice daily)
- After some time, you may begin to see some white molds inside. Everything is OK if the mold is white. However, if you notice any green or black mold, you must discontinue the process and start all over again. It means you must have gotten something wrong. This is why it is important that you do not allow any foreign agent to enter.
- On day 4, strain your fermented contents into a large bowl.
- Get a good quantity of egg shells.
- Wash the eggs shells and boil to kill harmful bacteria.
- Blend the egg shells to a paste by adding a little water as you blend.

- Now add the egg shell paste into the bowl with the fermented contents.
- Then add molasses in a ratio of 3:1 (molasses forming 1 part of the mixture).
- Your MVC is ready

Molasses is used as a preservative and a tonic

Dosage: *20ml to a liter of water*

PREPARATION OF ORGANIC MULTIVITAMIN SYRUP

You want to promote your birds' growth and help them to effectively utilize all the nutrients in their feed? Then you need to give them organic multivitamins.

Ingredients:

1. Carrots
2. Garden eggs
3. Cucumber
4. Ripe Pawpaw
5. Water melon
6. Oranges

HOW TO MAKE ORGANIC MULTIVITAMIN SYRUP

- Get all items in large quantities and in equal proportions.
- Peel the back of the oranges and water melon.
- Cut all the fruits into small pieces and blend adding a little water as you blend.
- Pour content into a large bucket.
- Add water twice the volume of blended contents.
- Cover with a breathable mesh and hold with a rubber band.
- Store away from sunlight for 72 hours.
- On the fourth day, strain contents in a large bowl.
- Add Molasses in a ratio of 3:1 (molasses forming 1 part of the mixture).
- Your organic multivitamin syrup is ready.

PREPARATION OF APPLE CIDER VINEGAR

Apple Cider Vinegar for poultry is cheap and highly effective in the prevention of disease outbreak in poultry farms. As a matter of fact, it's effectiveness in managing chicken health makes it the farmer's delight. ACV is completely natural and nontoxic. It is rich in vitamins, minerals and potassium.

Here are some of its benefits:

- It improves digestion of feed and nutrients.
- It helps to break down minerals and fats.
- It promotes protein assimilation, hence, promoting growth and wellness.
- Positive effect on Food Conversion Ratio (FCR).
- Improves birds' stamina.
- It is a good stimulant in egg formation in early life of pullets.
- It enhances growth.
- Prevents diseases outbreak.

DiY Agric © 2020

As you can see, there are lots of benefits to talk about and I believe you want to have all these benefits on your farm too. Let's make a list of everything you need to prepare your ACV.

Ingredients:

1. Red apple
2. Glass or plastic jar
3. Rubber band
4. Breathable mesh
5. Water
6. Wooden spoon

How to prepare your Apple Cider Vinegar (ACV)

- Buy red apples (2 for 1 liter of water).
- Peel off the back, slice thinly.
- Fill your jar with the required volume of water (preferably, don't fill the jar up).
- Pour the apple cuts into the desired volume of water (not chlorinated water).
- Cover with a breathable mesh and use rubber band to hold it tight.
- Stir once a day with a wooden spoon because the apples above the water level will grow fungi if you do not stir it.
- Use wooden spoon because metals can react with the fermentation process

- Once the sliced apple sink you can either take them out of the jar, or leave them in there. That should happen in about 2 to 3 weeks
- Total fermentation is 6 weeks

_Dosage__: 1ml to 1liter of water_

Caution: You need to take note of this warnings before you begin to use your ACV.

- Do not top the ACV with water after fermentation
- Your Apple Cider Vinegar burns fat, so do not give your birds too often. Twice a week is appropriate
- Also, to be sure that the ACV you have produced is exactly what you want, do not tamper with the fermentation process, only stir with wooden spoon.

DiY Agric © 2020

PREPARATION OF MOLASSES

Molasses simply put is refined sugarcane juice. It is thick and brownish-black in colour. It can be used as a sweetener, tonic and preservative for other organic concoctions. All you need to produce molasses is sugar cane. Let's quickly get into the process.

How to make molasses

- Get a large quantity of sugarcane
- Crush them in a mill to extract the juice
- Strain juice into a bowl so that other particles are removed
- Pour the juice into a large drum or pot, depending on the quantity, heat it up or boil it.
- While cooking it keep stirring it so that it does not stick to the bottom of the pot or drum.
- The boiling of the juice will produce a crystallization of the sugar allowing it to form the basest stage of the Molasses.

- Once the colour turns to blackish-brown and it is quite thick, bring it down and allow it to cool.
- Store in bottles.
- Your molasses is ready.

PREPARATION OF TAGIRI

Tagiri (Christmas Melon) is interestingly known to ward off viral diseases in poultry. That is, with Tagiri, diseases like Newcastle Disease, Marek's Disease, and Infectious Bursal Disease (IBD) can be combated and prevented completely. However, it is important to know how this wonderful bulb can be used effectively without any complications. As with synthetic drugs, caution must be taken in the use of organic fighting agents like Tagiri, as this is the only way to maximize the benefits of organic poultry farming without regrets. But do not worry; everything will be highlighted in this book.

Ingredients Required to Prepare Tagiri Extract

1. Tagiri bulbs (1kg Tagiri for 2 liters of water)
2. Water
3. Other Materials Required
4. A jar or container with cover
5. Knife (to cut the Tagiri bulbs into pieces)
6. A calibrated container to measure the volume of water to be used

7. A weighing balance to measure the weight of the Tagiri bulbs

How to Make Tagiri Extract

- Get some Tagiri bulbs
- Peel off the green back
- Cut the Tagiri into pieces
- Measure water that is twice the weight of the Tagiri cuts in liters (i.e. ratio 1:2)
- Pour the water into your jar or container
- Add the Tagiri cuts
- Cover the jar/container with a breathable mesh and use rubber band to hold it tight
- Keep in a cool dark room and allow the Tagiri cuts to ferment inside the water for 7 days
- Do not tamper with the process
- On day 7, strain the Tagiri water into a bigger container, and then blend the Tagiri cuts and the seeds
- Add the blended Tagiri into the Tagiri liquid that was strained earlier
- At this stage, you cannot add fresh water
- The Tagiri extract is ready at this stage but we are left with one concern – preservation. You can either choose to cover the jar containing the Tagiri extract and refrigerate or preserve with molasses.

DiY Agric © 2020

How to Preserve Tagiri with Molasses

Add 1-part molasses to 3 parts Tagiri extract. That is, 1:3. If you have 3 liters of Tagiri extract, you will need to add 1 liter of molasses to preserve it. Note that you do not need to refrigerate after adding molasses to the extract.

Tagiri Preservation (Refrigeration VS Molasses)

While you can skip the use of molasses and preserve your Tagiri extract by refrigeration, it is important to mention that molasses keep the Tagiri extract longer than refrigeration. While it is advisable to use up refrigerated Tagiri extract within 1 month, molasses-preserved extract can stay up to 4 months. The choice of preservation method also depends on the quantity of Tagiri extract you have produced and how long it will take to use it up. In any case, the fresher the Tagiri extract is, the better. So, make sure to produce the quantity you will be able to use up before the extract expires.

Dosage of Tagiri Extract:

30ml of Tagiri extract to 1 Liter of water.

Use of Tagiri and Age of chicken

Never use Tagiri extract for pullets and breeders above 14 weeks or layers in production.

Tagiri extract is completely safe for birds before 14 weeks

Tagiri extract can be given to day-old chicks in the form of vaccine to ward off Newcastle disease, Marek's disease, etc.

Tagiri is one of the greatest recent discoveries in organic poultry farming and its power cannot be overemphasized. I hope that you are also able to digest this article and use Tagiri for the benefit of your organic chickens. You will find out how cost-effective organic poultry farming can be with Tagiri when you substitute vaccines for Tagiri extract.

PREPARATION OF LACTIC ACID BACTERIA (LAB)

Lactic Acid Bacteria (LAB) are probiotics and additives used to boost the immune system of poultry birds. It also helps in weight gain, better feed conversion (FCR) etc. After producing LAB, you will be able to use it for your birds and other livestock.

Ingredients:

1. Rice
2. Milk
3. Water

How to produce Lactic Acid Bacteria

- Get about 3 cups of rice. Ultimately, the quantity of rice depends on the volume of LAB you want to produce.
- Wash the rice in a bowl, **do not throw away the water because that is what we need in this production**
- Strain the water. Because the rice itself is not needed for the process, you can cook the rice and eat.
- Now, pour the water into a jar or small plastic bucket.

- Cover the bucket or jar with a breathable mesh and hold with a rubber band.
- Store away for 5 to 7 days
- After 7 days, the content of the jar is expected to have separated into 3 layers; a thin layer of dirt at the top, a somewhat clear water in the middle, and a thick gathering at the bottom
- Use a spoon to scoop away the thin layer at the top. Alternatively, if you have a big syringe, you can insert it, allowing the head to be in the second layer, and draw out the clear liquid in the layer only.
- If you have used the first method, carefully strain the second layer into a bowl. That is the part we need, then throw away the thick layer at the bottom.
- Add 10 parts liquid milk (you can buy 900g of powdered milk and dissolve in water) into the bowl containing the fermented rice wash. The preferred milk is full cream milk.
- For the volume of milk, if your fermented rice wash water is 1 liter, add 10 liters of liquid milk to it.
- Stir vigorously for some seconds
- Use a paint bucket for this and make a little hole at the top of the cover to allow the microbes that will multiply to breathe. The hole should not be more than half an inch. Then you should cover the hole with a mesh. Preferably, make a hole with a biro/pen case, insert it and cover with a breathable mesh.
- Do not allow flies or insects into the contents as they will destroy the process. Also keep away from sunlight

- Allow for another 7 days
- After 7 days you will notice a thick white hard substance called curd, take it out.
- This curd can be mixed with feed and fed to your organic chickens and livestock. Let's continue with the main target.
- Strain the liquid into a bowl
- The liquid at this stage can be used as an odour killer in your pen or septic tank at home
- Now, add an equal amount of molasses to the new liquid
- That is, if you have 1 liter of LAB add 1 liter of molasses to it. This is for preservation, otherwise refrigerate.
- Now to use our LAB for our birds we must activate it.

To activate, dilute 1 liter of LAB in 10 liters of water

Dosage to administer after activation: _10ml to 1 liter of water_

ORGANIC DAILY CHART FOR BROILERS

DAY	ORGANIC MEDICATION
1-3	LAB, Tagiri, Ginger & Garlic Extract
4	Clean water
5	Cayenne(dry)/Habanero (fresh)
6	Clean water
7-9	LAB, Tagiri, Ginger & Garlic Extract, MVC in the evening
10	Clean water
11	Bitter Leaf extract & Cayenne/Habanero
12	Clean water
13-15	LAB, Tagiri, Ginger & Garlic Extract, MVC in the evening
16	Clean water
17	Turmeric & Black pepper, Bitter leaf extract. MVC in the evening
18	Turmeric & Black pepper, Bitter leaf extract. MVC in the evening
19	Clean water

DiY Agric © 2020

Day	Medication
20-22	LAB, Tagiri, Ginger & Garlic Extract. MVC in the evening
23	Clean water
24	Scent Leaf extract & Cayenne/Habanero pepper
25	Turmeric & Black pepper
26	Turmeric & Black pepper
27	Clean water
28-30	LAB, Tagiri, Ginger & Garlic Extract. MVC in the evening
31	Clean water
32	Fresh Habanero pepper
33	Clean water
34	Turmeric & Black pepper
35	Turmeric & Black pepper
36	Clean water
37-38	LAB, Tagiri, Ginger & Garlic Extract, MVC.
39	Clean water
40	Fresh habanero pepper
41	Clean water
42	LAB, Tagiri, Ginger & Garlic Extract, MVC in the evening

NOTE: Give Tagiri early morning shot to birds from day 1 to 6 weeks, **except on days when Tagiri is among the medications to be given**.

For example, Day 1-3 says LAB, Tagiri, Ginger & Garlic extract.

In this case, Tagiri is listed on day 1-3 therefore, you can rule out giving Tagiri early morning shot

Second example

Day 5 says Canyenne pepper (dry)/Habanero(fresh)

You can see that Tagiri is not on the list for that day's menu so you need to give the birds Tagiri early morning shot and so on...

Dosage: 30ml to 2 liters 100 birds and 60ml to 4 liters 200 birds (serve as vaccine)

Dosage of LAB is 10ml to 1 liter of water

NOTE: From 4 weeks give ACV once a week. 1ml to a liter of water

From 7 weeks: Give Ginger + Garlic once a week to continue boosting their immune system.

20ml each to a liter of water

Give bitter leaves extract once a week to prevent Coccidiosis.

20ml to a liter of water (preventive dosage)

DiY Agric © 2020

Give Turmeric + Black pepper once a week to aid digestion.

Dosage: 1g per kg

For dry ingredients, use 1 teaspoon (4.2 grams) to a liter of water

From 6 weeks continue to give LAB 4 times a week 20ml to a liter of water

SOME IMPORTANT QUESTIONS YOU SHOULD ASK YOURSELF IF YOUR ORGANIC MEDICATION IS NOT EFFECTIVE

Some people have had issues with their organic medications in the past, and this is why you need to pay close attention to the procedures given. In any case, the problem is usually because you missed something important during the preparation. Here are some of the questions you can ask yourself to get back on track.

1. During blending/grinding, were the ingredients adulterated?
2. How thick is the juice extract?
3. What ml did you use as preventive and curative dosage?
4. Were the birds eating and drinking before you started the administration of the medications?
5. When you serve the birds the medications, do you just dump the water there and move away or you stay and observe that all the birds drink from the medicated water?

DiY Agric © 2020

SIDE NOTE: If the birds are too weak to drink, use a syringe (without the needle) to give them the medications manually, 3 times daily (10 ml each time)

To a large extent, a bird's overall health depends on the health of its intestines. Hence, healthy substances like bitter leaf and scent leaf (basil) extracts should be given at least once a week to help repair their fragile intestines. By so doing, poultry diseases such as coccidiosis that take place in the intestine can be arrested.

FINAL NOTE

Organic poultry farming is possible and worth exploring. You may experience some difficulties in the beginning, especially in finding some of the leaves and roots, but nothing comes easy. Once you are determined, you will find a solution to getting your ingredients, and once that is settled, all you need is to stick to this guide and enjoy your business.

My advice is that you get most of your herbs and spices ready before you go organic, because once started, you have to keep your birds fully protected with these medications (as outlined in the chart) for the best results.

Here's the good news. Even if you are not able to go 100% organic in the beginning due to scarcity of some leaves and roots, the knowledge in this book will help you to substitute some synthetic drugs with common organic remedies. And that's a lot of savings for you.

BONUSES

Sample Financial Expenditure (2018)

ESTIMATES FOR RAISING 100 BIRDS

Price of DOC= N260 x 100 = N26,000

Starter Feed = 6 bags (150kg)

N3450 x 6bags = N20,700

(For 4 weeks)

Finisher Feed = 18bags (450kg)

N3,350 x 18 bags = N60,300

Research has proven that a broiler chicken needs an average of 6kg of quality feed to attain 3kg live weights within 8 weeks, with best managerial practices. This works for me and can work for you too.

DiY Agric © 2020

Summary of expenditure:

DOC = N26,000

Chick Starter = 20,700

Finisher= 60,300

Organic medications = N4,000 (if you are producing your ingredients)

Charcoal = N2,000

Kerosene =500

Firewood = N500

Wood shaving = 2,000

Newspaper = 300

Miscellaneous = 4,000

Total = N120,300

Mortality may be up to 4% - 5%

Expected live weights = 2kg to 3.5kg

So we make our calculations based on 95 birds

The selling price of birds depends on the location

We will use N1700

DiY Agric © 2020

So N1700 x 95 = N161,500

Expenditures = N120,300

Profit = N41,200

This can only be achieved if there is good management and adequate biosecurity in place.

SAMPLE FEED FORMULA

BROILER STARTER FEED (1000 KG)

MAIZE ------------ 550kg

SOYA MEAL -------- 160kg

GNC ------ 130kg

WHEAT OFFAL ------- 113.6kg

FISHMEAL (72%) ------- 19.8kg

METHIONINE -------- 1kg

LYSINE ---------- 0.2kg

LIMESTONE ---------- 8.6kg

BONE MEAL ---------- 11.8kg

STARTER PREMIX -------- 2.5kg

SALT -------- 2.5kg

Total: 1000kg

BROILER FINISHER FEED FORMULATION (1000KG)

MAIZE -------558kg

SOYA MEAL ------86kg

GNC ------146kg

WHEAT OFFAL-------150kg

FISHMEAL 29.35kg

METHIONINE -------0.65kg

LYSINE --------1kg

LIMESTONE -------12.5kg

BONE MEAL---------11.5kg

FINISHER PREMIX-------2.5kg

SALT-------2.5kg

Total 1000kg

Opeyemi Afeluyi

I WISH YOU SUCCESS!!!

I WISH YOU SUCCESS!!!

I WISH YOU SUCCESS!!

remember DiY-Agric ©

DiY Agric © 2020

Printed in Great Britain
by Amazon